The Chiappa Sisters and friends Family Summer Recipes

By

The Chiappa sisters and friends

Copyright Protection

All text, image and other materials contained or displayed in this book are proprietary and constitute valuable intellectual property. No materials from any part of this book are authorized or intended by us to be downloaded, transmitted, broadcast, reproduced or in any other way used or otherwise disseminated in any form to any person or entity, unless said person or entity has license to do so. All unauthorized duplication or any other use of materials from this book, including, but not limited to, use on other Web sites, or in offers to resell products using similar names or descriptions, shall constitute intentional infringement(s) of our intellectual property and shall further constitute a violation of our trademarks, copyrights, and other rights. Without further notice we will prosecute fully allowed by law.

If you are thinking about borrowing (stealing) someone else's material. You should read this!

Copyright laws provide for penalties of up to $150,000 per infringement. If you want to share the recipes in this book just buy another copy. How would you feel if you didn't get paid for the work you did? Don't screw us over because not only will we find out, but the man upstairs is watching! Our books are affordably priced for everyone to buy. This is how we make our living!

Copyright © The Chiappa sisters and friends 2017.

Table of content

Introduction Pg. 13

Tasty Grape Salad Pg. 15

Grilled Shrimp with Garlic & Herbs Pg. 18

Cheesy Potato Casserole Pg. 21

Watermelon Lemonade Pg. 23

Grilled Lemon Salmon Pg. 26

Parmesan Corn On The Cob Pg. 30

Hot Dog Chili Pg.33

Oregano & Lemon Pork Kebabs Pg. 36

Antipasto Salad Pg. 40

Mango Sorbet Pg. 42

Caribbean Breeze drink Pg. 44

Chickpea Salad Pitas Pg. 46

Spinach and Mushroom Pasta Bake Pg. 49

Blushing Rose Lemonade Pg. 53

Pineapple Buganda Pg. 56

Strawberry Coconut Salad Pg. 58

Coconut Chicken with a Tropical Mango Rum Sauce Pg.60

Dijon Sirloin Tips Pg. 65

Minty Onion Tomato Salad Pg. 69

Caribbean Grilled Burger with Pineapple Sauce Pg.71

Grilled Balsamic Eggplant Pg. 75

Lavender and Lemon Poached Chicken Breasts pg. 78

Seared Tuna in Wasabi Sauce Pg. 81

Nectarine Upside Down Cake Pg. 85

Heirloom Tomato, Mozzarella and Basil Side Dish Pg. 89

Pepperoni Pasta Salad Pg.91

Butternut Squash Lasagna Pg.94

Cape Cod on a Summer's day drink Pg.101

Carrots with Apricots Pg. 103

Pork Chops with Pineapple Green Onion Relish Pg. 107

Summer Grilled Chicken Breast Sandwich with Avocado Cilantro Pg.111

Tangy Herb Potato Salad Pg.115

Seaside Stuffed Summer Squash Pg.118

Sautéed Fresh Fig and Almond Dessert Pg. 121

Cucumber-Lime Agua Fresca Pg. 124

Turkey and Sweet Potato Wraps Pg. 127

Agua Velvet Pg. 131

Tropical Pineapple Banana Ice Cream Pg.133

Honolulu Lulu Pg. 136

Grilled Apple Spice Trout Fillets Pg.138

Watermelon Basil Vinaigrette Pg. 142

Ravioli with Asparagus, Mint & Mascarpone Pg. 144

Wild Mango and Mustard Seed Salad Pg. 147

Grilled Rum Peaches With Mascarpone Cheese & Orange Blossom Pg.150

Battered and Baked Sage Leaves Pg.153

Caramel Grilled Pineapple Sundaes Pg. 156

Coffee Barbecue Sauce Pg. 158

White Cactus Pg. 159

Pepper Jack Mac Salad Pg. 161

Maple Pepper Steaks pg. 164

Alouette Potato Salad Pg. 167

Seafood Risotto Pg. 170

Crown of Roses Pg.173

Chocolate Eclair Dessert Pg. 175

Southern Style Cinnamon Honey Chicken Pg. 178

Garlic Ricotta Stuffed Mushrooms Pg. 182

Blackberry Coffee Cake Pg. 185

Five-Spices Chicken Wings Pg. 189

Tomato Beef Chow Mein Pg. 192

Apple Juice Frosty Pg. 197

The Blizzard Pg. 199

Good Thyme Lamb Chops Pg. 201

Dedicated to Kassidy and Jocelyn..

Shopping lists...

Shopping lists...

Introduction.

Hi you might know us as the Chiappa Family, but did you know we hail from Long Island, New York? You might have seen our many books on amazon and many other websites, seen our newspaper articles or caught our interviews on T.V. or radio but the truth is we started out in humble beginnings. We worked hard to become a house hold name. We grew up in Commack and Kings Park N.Y. We first lived in a 200-year-old house on Church Street that was next to a V.F.W. hall in Kings Park. Our first experience in the Food Industries was selling Lemonade to the little grey-haired ladies that used to come play bingo at the V.F.W. next to where we lived. By the time we were teenagers we were cooking and serving in some of Long Island's hottest eatery's. We learned our skills by working hard, taking advice but most of all being creative.

Some of our best memories of Long Island, are skating at the Commack roller rink, going to Adventureland, and picnics in my grandmother's back yard. Through food we can relive our best childhood memories. Who doesn't recall the first time that ate a chili dog at a ball game or have an ice cream soda on a hot Summer's day? This book is dedicated to Long Island Summers that we will never forget. In this book you will find some of our top recipes that you can use to make your own lasting Summer memories.

Tasty Grape Salad

Ingredients

2 lbs green seedless grapes

2 lbs red seedless grapes

8 ounces sour cream

8 ounces cream cheese, softened

1/2 cup granulated sugar

1 teaspoon vanilla extract, to taste

Topping Ingredients

1 cup brown sugar, packed, to taste

1 cup crushed pecans, to taste

Directions

Wash and stem grapes.

Set aside.

Mix sour cream, cream cheese, white sugar and vanilla by hand until blended.

Stir grapes into mixture, and pour in large serving bowl.

For topping: Combine brown sugar, and crushed pecans.

Sprinkle over top of grapes to cover completely.

Chill overnight.

Tasty Grape Salad

Grilled Shrimp with Garlic & Herbs

Ingredients

2 lbs extra large shrimp, peeled deveined

1 teaspoon paprika

1 tablespoon sliced fresh garlic

1 teaspoon italian seasoning

1 tablespoon fresh lemon juice

2 tablespoons olive oil

1/2 teaspoon black pepper

1 teaspoon basil

1 tablespoon brown sugar

Directions

Mix all ingredient in a bag and marinate for 20 minutes in the refrigerator. Prepare grill to high heat and grill for 5-6 minutes turning to char all sides.

Grilled Shrimp with Garlic & Herbs

Cheesy Potato Casserole

Ingredients

2 lbs frozen hash browns (I use the diced kind)

1/2 cup butter

1 (10 1/2 ounce) can cream of chicken soup

1 cup sour cream

1 cup shredded cheddar cheese

1/4 cup diced onion

salt and pepper, to taste

Directions

Defrost potatoes, melt butter, and mix together all ingredients.

Bake at 350 degrees for 1 hour in a 9x13 baking dish.

Cheesy Potato Casserole

Watermelon Lemonade

Ingredients

8 cups cubed seedless watermelon

2 (12 ounce) cans frozen lemonade concentrate

4 cups water

Directions

Place watermelon in a blender or food processor.

Cover and blend on medium speed until smooth.

Place lemonade concentrate and water in a large pitcher or punch bowl.

Add watermelon.

Mix well.

Garnish with additional watermelon if desired.

Watermelon Lemonade

Grilled Lemon Salmon

Ingredients

2 teaspoons fresh dill

1/2 teaspoon pepper

1/2 teaspoon salt

1/2 teaspoon garlic powder

1 1/2 lbs salmon fillets

1/4 cup packed brown sugar

1 chicken bouillon cube, mixed with

3 tablespoons water

3 tablespoons oil

3 tablespoons soy sauce

4 tablespoons finely chopped green onions

1 lemon, thinly sliced

2 slices onions, separated into rings

Directions

Sprinkle dill, pepper, salt and garlic powder over salmon.

Place in shallow glass pan.

Mix sugar, chicken bouillon, oil, soy sauce, and green onions.

Pour over salmon.

Cover and chill for 1 hour, turn once.

Drain and discard marinade.

Put on grill on med heat, place lemon and onion on top.

Cover and cook for 15 minutes, or until fish is done.

Grilled Lemon Salmon

Parmesan Corn On The Cob

Ingredients

1 cup butter, melted

1/4 cup grated parmesan cheese

1/2 teaspoon Italian seasoning

6 ears corn

water, to boil corn

1/2 cup water

Salt

Directions

Mix first 3 ingredients.

Set aside.

Bring water to boil, add corn; boil for 8 minutes.

Drain well.

Brush with butter mix.

Salt to taste.

Parmesan Corn On The Cob

Hot Dog Chili

Ingredients

2 lbs ground chuck

1 (42 ounce) can tomato juice

1 jar chili powder (at least 3 oz - I use more)

1 grated onion

1 tablespoon sugar

1 teaspoon garlic powder

1 tablespoon salt

1 tablespoon paprika (more if needed for color-later)

Ketchup

Directions

Take out ground chuck 30 minutes ahead of time (this warms it up for your hand) Using gloved hand, squish in 1st 8 ingredients until you can no longer see tomato juice.

Start cooking on med to med high, stirring, watching till it starts cooking and turn down to simmer, stirring occasionally.

Simmer about 30 minutes to 1 hour, or longer, You really can't over cook.

Add ketchup, a few squirts at a time for color and flavor.

Stir thru, adjust any seasoning you feel fit.

Hot Dog Chili

Oregano & Lemon Pork Kebabs

Ingredients

1 lb lean pork loin, cut into 1 inch cubes

Marinade

1/2 cup lemon juice

1 tablespoon oil

2 teaspoons dried oregano

1 teaspoon rosemary sprig

1 garlic clove, crushed

1/4-1/2 teaspoon fresh ground black pepper

Choose 2 or 3 from a selection of vegetables

1 medium red pepper, cut into large chunks

1 medium zucchini, cut into 3/8 inch thick slices

8 grape tomatoes

1 medium onion, cut into large chunks

8 medium white mushrooms

Directions

For the marinade combine all ingredients in a resalable plastic bag or non-reactive bowl.

Trim the pork of all visible fat and cut into 1 inch cubes. Place cubes in bag and marinate in the fridge for 30 minutes. (You can also toss the vegetables in if you like. Mushrooms and zucchini are especially good in absorbing the flavor.).

In the meantime, soak wooden skewers in water.

Wash and cut vegetables for kebabs.

Thread kebabs alternating between the pork cubes and vegetables. Depending on the size of your pork cubes and the length of the skewers, you will have 1 large or 2 small skewers per person.

Place on indoor or outdoor grill and cook for 8 to 10 minutes.

Oregano & Lemon Pork Kebabs

Antipasto Salad

Ingredients

1 (16 ounce) package rotini pasta

1 (15 ounce) can garbanzo beans, rinsed and drained

1 (3 1/2 ounce) package sliced pepperoni, halved

1 (2 1/4 ounce) can sliced ripe olives, drained

1/2 cup diced sweet red pepper

1/2 cup diced green pepper

4 medium fresh mushrooms, sliced

2 cloves garlic, minced

2 teaspoons dried basil

2 teaspoons salt

1/2 teaspoon dried oregano

1/2 teaspoon pepper

1/4 teaspoon cayenne pepper

1 cup olive oil

2/3 cup lemon juice

Directions

Cook the pasta according to package directions; drain and rinse with cold water.

Place in a large salad bowl.

Add the next 12 ingredients; mix well.

In a jar with tight-fitting lid, shake oil and lemon juice.

Pour over salad and toss.

Cover and refrigerate 6 hours or overnight.

Stir before serving.

Antipasto Salad

Mango Sorbet

Ingredients

1 mango, ripe

3 tablespoons powdered sugar

Peel the mango. Cut the flesh from the stone and dice it. Place in a zip-lock bag, close it (be careful to keep the air out) and freeze for at least 4 hours.

Take the bag out of the freezer and allow to thaw for about 20 minutes at room temperature.

Put slightly thawed mango pieces into a tall bowl (or the bowl of your blender), add powdered sugar and puree the mango into a creamy sorbet using a hand-held blender (or simply blend in your blender).

Mango Sorbet

Caribbean Breeze drink

Ingredients

1 ounce light rum

1 ounce coconut rum

3 ounces pineapple juice, chilled

3 ounces cranberry juice, chilled

Directions

Fill a tall glass with ice pour ingredients. garnish with a cherry and enjoy!

Caribbean Breeze drink

Chickpea Salad Pitas

Ingredients

1 (16 ounce) can chickpeas

1/2 cucumber, diced (peeled if you like)

1/2 red pepper, diced

1/2 red onion, finely chopped

2 tablespoons olive oil

1 1/2 teaspoons balsamic vinegar

1/2 teaspoon garlic powder

1/2 teaspoon oregano

1/4 teaspoon fresh ground pepper

sea salt, to taste

lemon juice, to taste

2-3 whole wheat pita bread, cut in half

Directions

Combine all ingredients except pita's and lettuce. Chill at least 20 minutes before serving to let flavors mingle.

Cut pita bread in half, line both side with a few lettuce leaves.

Just before serving, spoon chickpea mixture into lettuce lined pita's; topping with feta and baby tomatoes if desired.

Chickpea Salad Pitas

Spinach and Mushroom Pasta Bake

Ingredients

8 ounces rotini pasta (I like to use whole wheat pasta)

2 teaspoons olive oil

1/4 cup chopped onion

1 teaspoon chopped garlic

4 ounces fresh mushrooms, sliced

5 ounces fresh Baby Spinach, cleaned & roughly chopped

2-3 tablespoons red wine

2 cups marinara sauce

1/2 teaspoon salt (to taste)

1/2 teaspoon black pepper (to taste)

1/4 teaspoon red pepper flakes, to taste (optional)

1/4 cup grated parmesan cheese

8 ounces mozzarella cheese, shredded

Directions

Preheat oven to 375°F Bring a large pot of water to a boil. Cook pasta according to package.

While water is boiling and pasta is cooking, heat oil in a large non-stick skillet over medium heat.

Add onion & saute until tender, about 5 minutes. Add garlic, cook 30 seconds.

Add mushrooms and cook until they release most of their liquid, about 5 minutes. Add spinach and wine and cook until spinach is wilted and most of the wine has evaporated, about 3 minutes.

Stir in marinara sauce, salt, and both peppers and stir until heated through. Add Parmesan cheese and stir to combine.

In a 2-quart casserole dish, cover the bottom with a thin layer of sauce. Add half the pasta, half the sauce, and half of the mozzarella. Repeat layers with remaining pasta , sauce, and mozzarella.

Bake for 20 minutes or until hot and bubbly.

Spinach and Mushroom Pasta Bake

Blushing Rose Lemonade

Ingredients

5 1/3 cups water

1 cup granulated sugar

1 1/3 cups fresh lemon juice (about 6 to 7 lemons)

2 1/2-3 1/2 teaspoons rose water (use the lesser amount for a more subtle flavor)

Directions

Combine water and sugar in a saucepan and heat over medium-low heat, stirring just until the sugar has dissolved.

Remove from heat and let cool.

Add to pitcher and stir in lemon juice.

Add rose water to taste.

Chill well before serving.

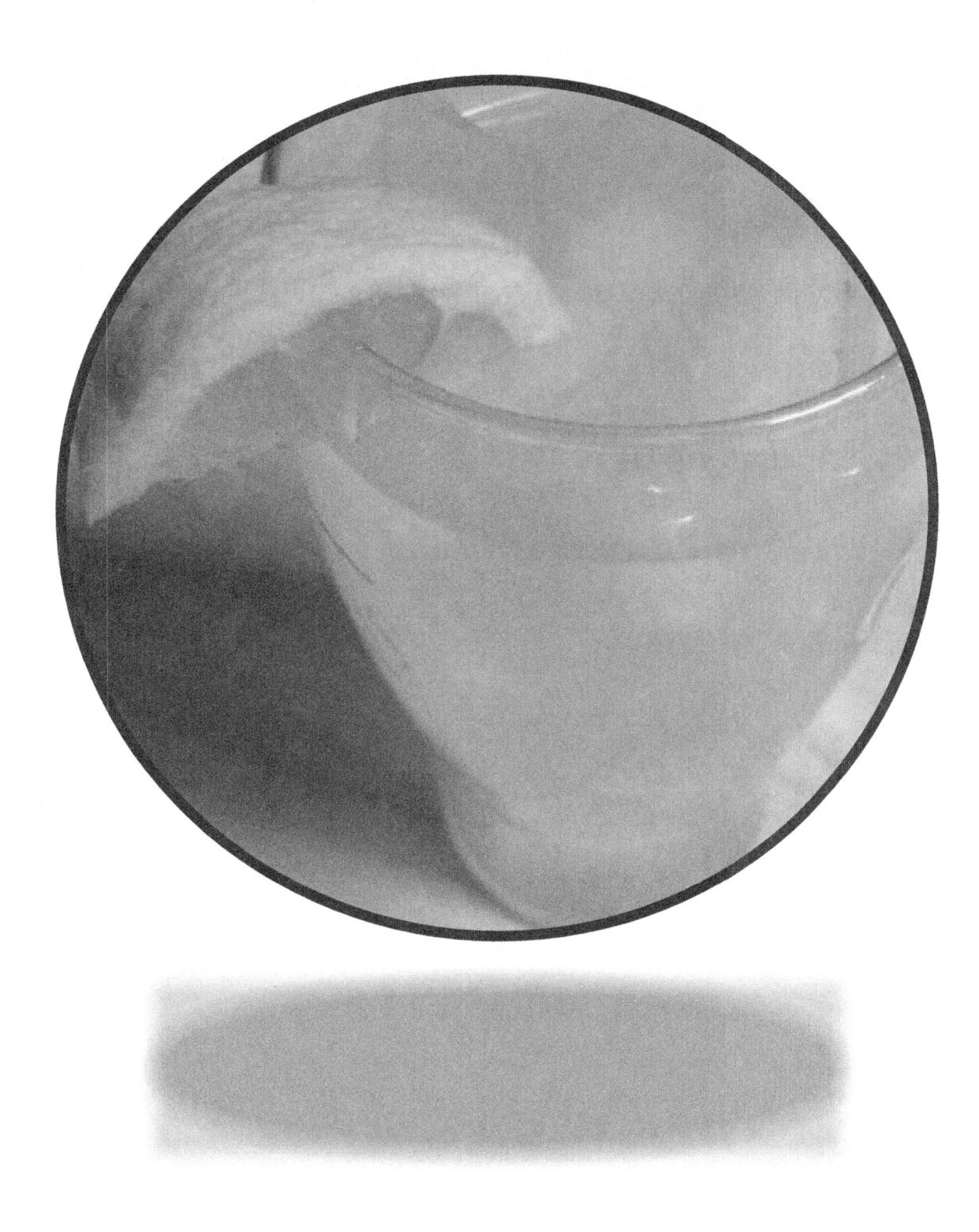

Blushing Rose Lemonade

Pineapple Buganda

Ingredients

2 cups fresh pineapple, very ripe and cut in small pieces

4 tablespoons brown sugar

1/2 cup cream or 1/2 cup coconut milk

6 ounces white rum

1 teaspoon vanilla extract

1 cup crushed ice

mint sprig, garnish

maraschino cherry, garnish

Directions

Blend until smooth and thick.

Serve with mint and a maraschino cherry in whiskey-sour glasses.

Pineapple Buganda

Strawberry Coconut Salad

Ingredients

2 cups strawberries

2 cups chopped pineapple

1/2 cup sugar

1/2 cup grated coconut

1 cup fresh orange juice

Directions

In a glass bowl, alternate layers of berries and pineapple, sprinkling sugar and coconut between each layer.

Pour the fresh orange juice over the top.

Serve cold.

Strawberry Coconut Salad

Coconut Chicken with a Tropical Mango Rum Sauce

Ingredients

Dusting for chicken

- 1/2 cup cornstarch
- 1/2 teaspoon grated nutmeg
- 1/2 teaspoon black pepper
- 1/4 teaspoon salt
- 1 1/2-2 lbs chicken breasts, cut into strips

Mango rum sauce

- 1/4 cup rum
- 2 large mangoes, peeled and diced
- 1/2 teaspoon grated nutmeg
- 1/2 teaspoon grated cinnamon
- 1/3 cup packed light brown sugar

1 large fresh lime juice, and zest or

1 large fresh lemon juice, and zest

1 teaspoon fresh grated ginger

1 teaspoon cornstarch

1/2 teaspoon scotch bonnet pepper (optional)

Coating for Chicken

3 egg whites

2 1/2 cups grated coconut

oil, to fry

Directions

Mix the first 4 ingredients together in a large container with a top. Add chicken pieces, toss till coated and set aside.

Place all Mango Rum Sauce ingredients in a blender or food processor and blend till smooth. Add to a pot and simmer over low heat for 10 minutes. Keep warm.

Whisk egg whites till frothy. Toss in chicken pieces till coated.

Place coconut in a bowl and dip each piece of chicken to coat with coconut.

Set aside.

Place enough oil to cover bottom of a large pan by 1/2 inch and heat to medium high.

Cook 1/2 the chicken at a time about 4-5 minutes each side. Do not over crowd the pan.

Drain cooked chicken on paper towels.

Place chicken on a serving platter serve with Mango Rum Sauce.

Coconut Chicken with a Tropical Mango Rum Sauce

Dijon Sirloin Tips

Ingredients

1 1/4lbs sirloin tip steaks, cubed

2 tablespoons butter or 2 tablespoons margarine

1 tablespoon cooking oil

3cups sliced fresh mushrooms

2 cloves garlic, minced

1/2cup beef broth

1/4cup white wine vinegar

1 1/2teaspoons soy sauce

2teaspoons Dijon mustard

2 teaspoons cornstarch

1/2cup whipping cream

hot cooked noodles

Directions

In a large skillet, brown the meat in butter and oil; transfer to an ungreased 2-quart baking dish.

In the same skillet, saute mushrooms and garlic until tender, about 3 minutes.

Pour over meat.

Cover and bake at 300 degrees for 1 1/2-2 hours or until meat is tender.

In a skillet, combine the broth, vinegar, and soy sauce; bring to a boil.

Boil for 2 minutes; set aside.

Combine mustard, cornstarch, and cream; stir into broth mixture.

Bring to a boil; boil for 2 minutes, stirring constantly.

Drain juices from baking dish into broth mixture.

Cook over medium heat, stirring constantly until thickened and bubbly.

Add beef mixture.

Serve over noodles.

Dijon Sirloin Tips

Minty Onion Tomato Salad

Ingredients

1 large walla walla onion, peeled and thinly sliced

4 tomatoes, sliced

1/2cup of fresh mint, minced

salt and pepper

Directions

Layer ingredients, cover and chill 2 hours or more.

Minty Onion Tomato Salad

Caribbean Grilled Burger with Pineapple Sauce

Ingredients

1 lb pineapple, cored

1 jalapeno pepper, split and seeded (wear gloves)

1 tablespoon molasses

1 lb lean ground sirloin, formed into 4 patties

4 tablespoons island jerk seasoning

1 1/2 cups iceberg lettuce, shredded

1/4 mango, peeled, seeded, cut in thin, matchlike sticks

4 mini sweet red peppers, sliced in rings

4 Kaiser rolls

Directions

Preheat grill on **HIGH** 10 minute.

Coat grill grate lightly with vegetable oil.

Puree pineapple, jalapeno and molasses in blender; set aside.

Coat beef patties with jerk seasoning (wear gloves).

Sear first side of burger on grill about 2 min; until meat has changed color 1/4 way up from bottom.

Turn and sear other side.

Turn meat back over.

Reduce heat to **MEDIUM** or **LOW** (Most burgers require **MEDIUM**; burgers thicker than 1 inch require **LOW**). Close lid.

Cook burgers to internal temp of 160 degrees.

Check by inserting thermometer halfway into thickest part of burger.

Remove from grill.

Place on rolls, top with sauce, lettuce, mango, and red bell pepper rings.

Caribbean Grilled Burger with Pineapple Sauce

Grilled Balsamic Eggplant

Ingredients

1 eggplant, peeled and sliced lengthwise in half the half again Check photo

Marinade

1 tablespoon fresh basil, chopped

2 tablespoons olive oil

2 tablespoons balsamic vinegar

1 teaspoon dried oregano

1 teaspoon dried parsley

2 garlic cloves, minced

1/2 teaspoon sugar

1/4 teaspoon black pepper

Salt

Directions

Add the marinade ingredients into a bag tossing to combine. Add the 4 quarters of the eggplant and marinade for 1 hour at room temperature or overnight in the refrigerator.

Preheat grill to high. Place the wedges on the grates reserving the marinade. Grill on hot oiled grates lowering heat to medium.

Brown on all three sides. Marking each side. Will be ready when easy to remove from grate. For more tender move to indirect heat and grill till desired. About 10 minutes.

Pour the reserved marinade over the hot eggplant.

Grilled Balsamic Eggplant

Lavender and Lemon Poached Chicken Breasts

Ingredients

2 boneless skinless chicken breasts

300ml good chicken stock

10 drops lavender, cooking essence or 1 teaspoon culinary lavender flowers

15 g butter

1 shallot, peeled and finely chopped

2 teaspoons cornflower

3 tablespoons creme fraiche

salt and pepper

1 tablespoon fresh lemon juice

fresh lavender flowers (to garnish)

Directions

Place the stock and lavender essence in a saucepan and bring to boil. Add the chicken breasts and return to boil and poach for 10-15 minutes until chicken is cooked through.

Remove the chicken to a dish and keep warm while making the sauce. Pour the stock into a jug.

Melt the butter in the pan and soften the shallot gently for 3-5 minutes. Sprinkle on the cornflower and stir to mix.

Gradually add the stock and stir while bringing to the boil. Simmer for 5 minutes then add the creme fraiche, salt and pepper. Simmer for a few minutes. Add lemon juice and season to taste.

Pour the sauce over the chicken, garnish each chicken breast with some lavender flowers and serve with wild rice or pasta; new potatoes and mange tout would also be good.

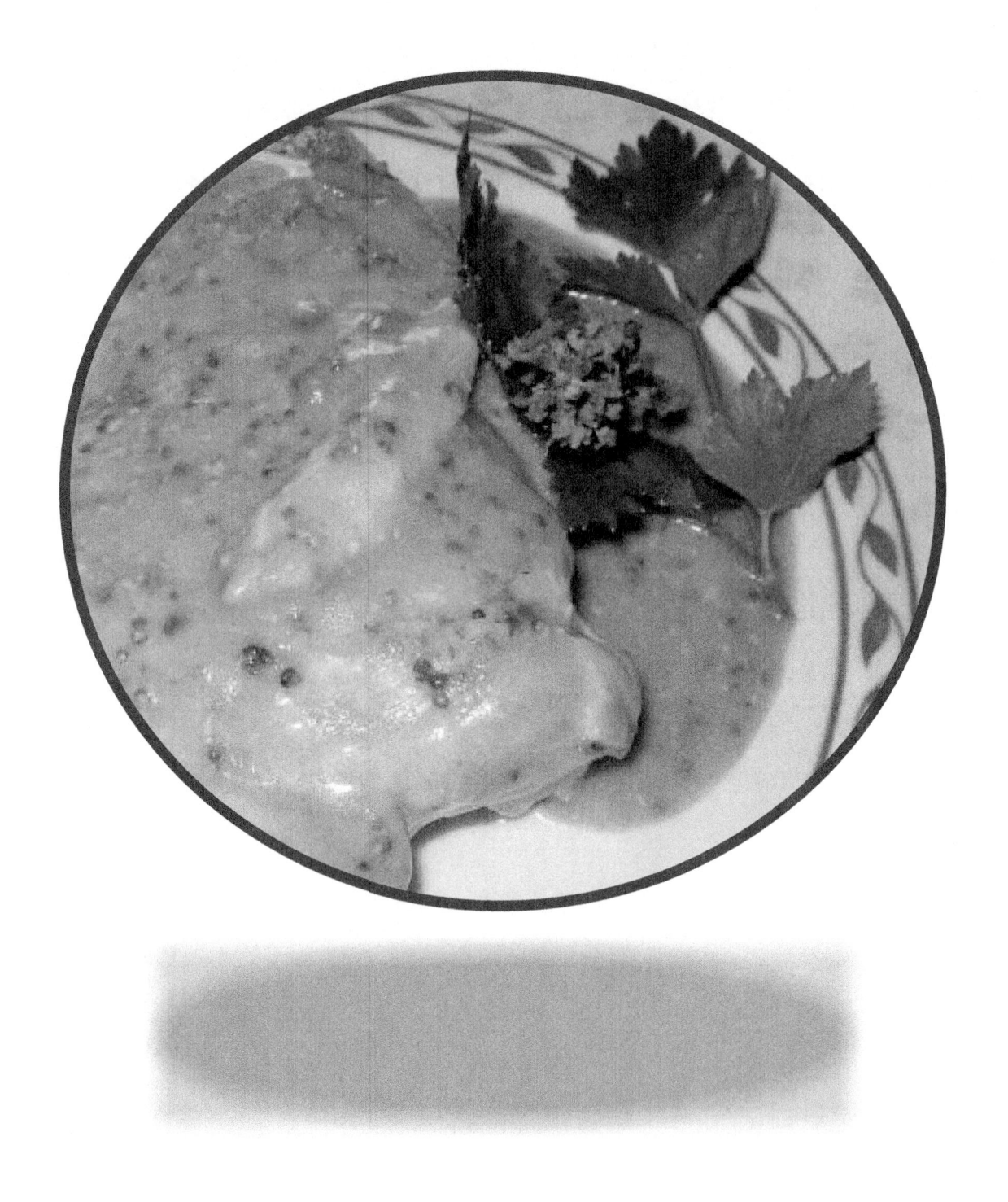

Lavender and Lemon Poached Chicken Breasts

Seared Tuna in Wasabi Sauce

Ingredients

1 1/4 cups white wine

2 tablespoons limes

1/4 cup onion, minced

1 piece fresh ginger, size of a quarter and crushed

1 garlic clove, left whole and but crushed

2 -4 tablespoons wasabi paste

1 tablespoon soy sauce

1/2 cup unsalted butter

1 cup fresh cilantro leaves or 1 cup fresh parsley

6 (6 ounce) tuna steaks

1 tablespoon olive oil

salt and pepper

Directions

Combine wine, lime, onion, ginger and garlic in a saucepan over medium heat. Simmer to reduce to about 2 tablespoons.

Place reduced sauce in blender with the butter, soy and wasabi and blend till smooth and butter is melted.

Place in a bowl.

Stir in cilantro.

Preheat grill high. It needs to be very hot!

Mix olive oil and 1 tablespoon sauce together. Brush tuna steaks with the sauce and oil mixture.

Grill for 90 seconds then turn and continue grilling for 90 seconds more.

If you just want the tuna seared remove from grill now. Otherwise continue grilling for 1 minute on each side again.

Serve tuna topped with the sauce.

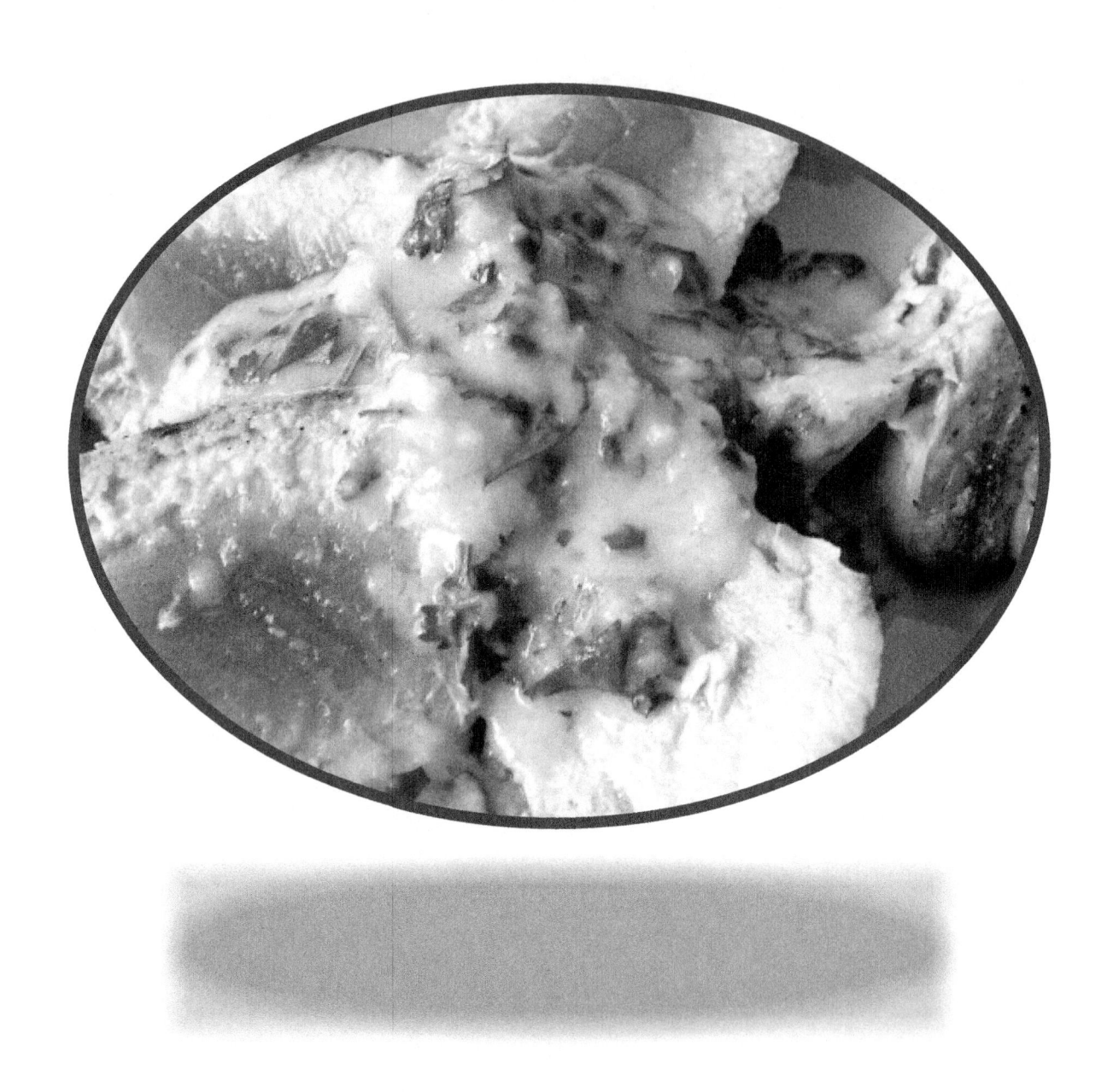

Seared Tuna in Wasabi Sauce

Nectarine Upside Down Cake

Ingredients

- 2 tablespoons butter or 2 tablespoons margarine
- 1/4 cup brown sugar, firmly packed
- 2-3 nectarines, peeled and sliced (no need to peel if nectarines are very soft)
- 1/2 cup butter or 1/2 cup margarine, softened
- 1 cup sugar
- 1/3 cup egg substitute or 2 large eggs
- 1/2 cup skim milk
- 1 teaspoon vanilla
- 1 1/4 cups all-purpose flour
- 1 teaspoon baking powder
- 1/2 teaspoon salt

Directions

Preheat oven to 350 degrees. Melt 2 tablespoons butter over medium heat. Add brown sugar and cook, stirring constantly, 2 minutes. Transfer to 9" round cake pan and spread evenly. Arrange nectarine slices over top in concentric circles in pan. If using large nectarines, you will only need 2 nectarines and will make two overlapping circles. If using smaller nectarines, you may need 3 nectarines and have more circles.

Beat butter until creamy. Add sugar and continue beating until light and fluffy. Add egg substitute or eggs and beat until blended. If using egg substitute, the mixture may look slightly curdled. Stir in milk and vanilla, blending well. Stir together dry ingredients; add to batter and mix on low speed just until blended. Batter is not very thick.

Spread batter evenly over nectarines. Bake cake until wooden pick tests clean, about 30-35 minutes. Let cool on wire rack 10 minutes, then invert onto serving platter. Cut into wedges to serve.

Nectarine Upside Down Cake

Heirloom Tomato, Mozzarella and Basil Side Dish

Ingredients

1 large heirloom tomato

2 pieces mozzarella cheese, round, cut 1/8 to 1/4 inch thick

4 basil leaves

2 tablespoons balsamic vinegar, drizzled to taste

2 tablespoons extra virgin olive oil, drizzled to taste

salt, to taste

Heirloom Tomato, Mozzarella and Basil Side Dish

Pepperoni Pasta Salad

Ingredients

1 (16 ounce) tri-color spiral pasta

2 pepperoni (or a pkg of slices, quartered)

1 bunch fresh broccoli

(8 ounce) package cheddar cheese

1 (14 ounce) can pitted black olives (small, drained)

1 large tomatoes

1 (16 ounce) Italian dressing

1 tablespoon Salad Supreme dry seasoning

Directions

Chop broccoli into bite size pieces and place into boiling water for about 2 minutes just until it turns bright green. Don't cook all the way.

Drain broccoli and set aside.

Bring rotini to a boil.

While rotini is boiling, chop the tomato, cheese, and pepperoni sticks.

Drain pasta and place into a large serving bowl.

Add pepperoni, broccoli, cheese, black olives and tomatoes.

Mix in the Italian dressing to desired texture and taste.

Sprinkle with Supreme Salad seasoning.

Chill in fridge.

Pepperoni Pasta Salad

Butternut Squash Lasagna

Ingredients

12 lasagna noodles

1 large butternut squash, about 3 lbs

2 tablespoons olive oil, divided

1/teaspoon salt

3 tablespoons butter, divided

2 cups chopped yellow onions (1 extra large onion)

1 1/2 lbs swiss chard, chopped, tough stems discarded

1/4 teaspoon salt

1/3 cup flour

1/4 teaspoon black pepper

1/4 teaspoon garlic salt

1/4 teaspoon ground nutmeg

1/4 teaspoon dried thyme

1/4 teaspoon ground dried sage

4 cups milk (2% is fine)

3/4 cup grated parmesan cheese

1 cup grated mozzarella cheese

4 tablespoons chopped green onions

Directions

Take the butternut squash and peel, seed, and cut it into 1/2-inch chunks.

Cook the lasagna noodles according to package directions.

Preheat oven to 450 degrees F.

In a large bowl, toss the butternut squash chunks with 1 tablespoon olive oil and 1/2 teaspoon salt, then place the chunks in a single layer on a large cookie sheet.

Roast the squash chunks for 30 minutes or until they're easily pierced with a fork, stirring after 15 minutes.

Remove chunks from the oven and mash squash with a food processor (or fork or potato masher) until almost smooth; set aside.

Lower the oven temperature to 375 degrees F.

In a large Dutch oven or saucepot, over medium heat melt together the remaining 1 tablespoon olive oil and 1 tablespoon of butter.

Add the chopped onion and cook for about 10 minutes or until golden, stirring often; add the Swiss chard and 1/4 teaspoon salt and cook until the chard is wilted and the liquid evaporates, which will take about 7 minutes.

Remove from heat and set aside.

In a large saucepan, melt the remaining butter over medium heat.

Whisk in the flour, pepper, garlic salt, nutmeg, thyme, and sage and cook for 1 minute while stirring constantly.

Gradually whisk in the milk until smooth and cook the sauce over medium-high heat until it boils and thickens slightly, stirring frequently.

Boil for an additional 2 minutes while stirring, then whisk in all but 2 tablespoons Parmesan cheese.

Remove the saucepan from heat.

In a 13" x 9" glass lasagna pan, spoon about 1/2 cup of the white sauce to cover the bottom of the pan.

Arrange 4 cooked lasagna noodles over the sauce, overlapping to fit; evenly spread all of the Swiss chard mixture over the noodles, top with about 1 cup white sauce, and sprinkle with about a 1/4 cup of mozzarella cheese.

Arrange 4 lasagna noodles on top, then about 1 cup white sauce and all butternut squash chunks, then a 1/4 cup of mozzarella cheese.

Top with remaining lasagna noodles, remaining white sauce, sprinkle with the chopped green onions and the remaining mozzarella cheese; sprinkle with the reserved 2 tablespoons Parmesan cheese.

Cover the lasagna pan with foil and bake at 375 degrees for 30 minutes, then remove the foil and bake for an additional 10 minutes or until hot and bubbly; let lasagna cool for 10 minutes before cutting, for easier serving.

Butternut Squash Lasagna

Cape Cod on a Summer's day drink

Ingredients

2 ounces vodka

1/2 lime, juice of

4 ounces cranberry juice

Directions

Shake with ice and serve on the rocks.

Cape Cod on a Summer's day drink

Carrots with Apricots

Ingredients

3 cup dried apricot

1 1/2 cups carrots, cut into 1/2 inch rounds

1 1/2 tablespoons water

1/2 teaspoon unsalted butter

1/8 teaspoon sugar

1 1/2 teaspoons fresh parsley (optional)

Directions

Cover apricots with hot water in a bowl and soak 1 1/2 hours.

Drain and pat dry.

Cut apricots into thin strips.

Combine next 4 ingredients in a heavy nonstick pan over medium heat.

Cover tightly, reduce heat to low and cook 12-15 minutes, or until carrots are just tender.

Add apricots and return to heat 1-2 minutes.

Serve carrots sprinkled with parsley if desired.

Carrots with Apricots

Pork Chops with Pineapple Green Onion Relish

Ingredients

Pork Chops

- 1 cup hoisin sauce
- 3 tablespoons rice wine vinegar
- 2 tablespoons soy sauce
- 4 garlic cloves, coarsely chopped
- 1 teaspoon sesame oil
- 16 thin pork chops (or 8 regular)

Pineapple-Green Onion Relish

- 6 green onions
- 2 tablespoons olive oil (plus a little for brushing)

1 medium pineapple, peeled and diced (or canned)

1 jalapeno pepper, finely chopped

2 tablespoons fresh lime juice

1 tablespoon honey

2 tablespoons cilantro, coarsely chopped

Directions

In a small bowl, combine hoisin, vinegar, soy, garlic and sesame oil.

Place the chops in a shallow pan and pour the marinade over them. Refrigerate 2-3 hours.

Preheat grill hot.

Brush the green onions with a little olive oil and season with salt and pepper.

Grill until almost cooked through, 4-5 minutes, and finely slice.

Place in a bowl and add the rest of the relish ingredients. Stir to combine.

Remove the chops from the marinade, shaking off the excess and discard the marinade.

Season chops with salt and pepper and grill until medium well.

Arrange on a large serving platter and serve with relish alongside.

Pork Chops with Pineapple Green Onion Relish

Summer Grilled Chicken Breast Sandwich with Avocado Cilantro

Ingredients

2 boneless skinless chicken breasts (6 oz.)

2 Kaiser rolls

3 tablespoons olive oil

2 tablespoons butter (for the rolls)

1 teaspoon Smokey paprika

1/4 teaspoon granulated garlic

iceberg lettuce leaf

sliced tomatoes

for the mayonnaise

1 avocado (seeded)

1 tablespoon fine diced garlic

2 tablespoons diced cilantro

2 tablespoons fresh lemon juice

1/2 teaspoon kosher salt

1/3 teaspoon white pepper powder

1/4 cup mayonnaise

Directions

Preheat your grill to 375 degrees.

Drizzle the Chicken with the Olive Oil and season with the Salt, Pepper, Paprika and the Graulated Garlic. Meanwhile in a bowl mix the Mayo Ingredients together with a fork leaving the mixture a little chunky.

Place the Chicken on the grill over medium direct heat and cook for approximatley 6 minutes per side depending on thickness.

Butter the rolls and toast them on the grill.

Remove the Rolls and spread some Avocado Mayo on both the top and bottom of each roll.

Add the Lettuce, Tomato, and the Chicken to the bottom bun.

Summer Grilled Chicken Breast Sandwich with Avocado Cilantro

Tangy Herb Potato Salad

Ingredients

5 lbs red potatoes (leave skin on or off, your preference)

1 cup mayonnaise (no miracle whip)

1 cup sour cream

1-2 tablespoon chopped fresh basil

3-5 tablespoons white vinegar (depending on taste)

salt and pepper

Directions

Cut potatoes in bite size chunks and boil in lightly salted water until tender.

In a large bowl mix all other ingredients.

Add potatoes to dressing and combine well.

Chill and serve!

Tangy Herb Potato Salad

Seaside Stuffed Summer Squash

Ingredients

1 lb large summer squash (if you can't find large ones, then use more smaller ones so the filling won't spill out)

1/2 cup green pepper, finely chopped

1/2 cup cheddar cheese, grated

1/2 cup sour cream

5 slices bacon, cooked and finely crumbled

1/2 cup sweet onion, finely minced

Directions

Cook squash in boiling water 10-12 minutes. Let cool a little and then slice lengthwise. Scoop out pulp.

Add remaining ingredients to pulp and mix well. Fill squash with mixture, and then place each squash half in a baking dish.

Bake 20 minutes in a 350 degree preheated oven.

Note: May be prepared up to 3 hours ahead of time and refrigerated until ready to bake.

Seaside Stuffed Summer Squash

Sautéed Fresh Fig and Almond Dessert

Ingredients

2 tablespoons butter

12 ripe fresh figs, halved lengthwise

1/4 cup brown

1 cup blanched slivered almond, toasted

heavy cream

Directions

Melt the butter in a large skillet over high heat.

Add the fig halves and sprinkle liberally with brown sugar.

Saute, turning the figs gently, until warmed through, about 4 minutes. Be careful not to let the butter/brown sugar burn, just caramelize.

Sprinkle with toasted almonds and garnish with heavy cream.

Sautéed Fresh Fig and Almond Dessert

Cucumber-Lime Agua Fresca

Ingredients

1 lb cucumber, cut into large chunks, plus slices for garnish

1/3 cup fresh lime juice, plus wedges for garnish

3 tablespoons sugar

1/8 teaspoon salt

4 cups cold water

Directions

In a blender, combine cucumbers, lime juice, sugar, salt and 4 cups of cold water. Blend until smooth. Pour mixture into a mesh strainer placed over a pitcher, pressing pulp to release as much liquid as possible. Discard pulp. Add enough ice to fill pitcher.

Garnish glasses with cucumber slices and lime wedges.

Cucumber-Lime Agua Fresca

Turkey and Sweet Potato Wraps

Ingredients

1 medium onion, finely chopped

1 medium sweet potato, peeled and cut into 1/2 inch pieces

1(14 ounce) canlow sodium reduced-fat chicken broth

3 tablespoons diced celery

1/2teaspoon salt

1teaspoon sage

1/4teaspoon black pepper

2 cups boneless cooked turkey, cubed

3/4cup seasoned stuffing mix

8(10 inch) whole wheat tortillas

2 cups shredded reduced-fat cheddar cheese

sliced jalapeno pepper (to garnish)

Directions

In a large saucepan, place onion, sweet potato, chicken broth, celery, salt, sage, and pepper, and bring to a simmer over medium heat, and cook 10 minutes, or until vegetables are softened.

Stir turkey and stuffing mix into vegetable mixture and heat on mediumm for 5 minutes, stirring often, or until heated through and mixture has thickened.

Heat 1 tortilla in a dry skillet over medium heat and sprinkle with 1/4 cup of cheese and top with 1/2 cup of the filling.

Allow cheese to melt for 10 seconds and remove from skillet.

Fold in two opposite sides of tortilla one inch each, and roll up.

Repeat with remaining tortillas.

Place seam side down on serving plate.

Top with jalapeno peppers.

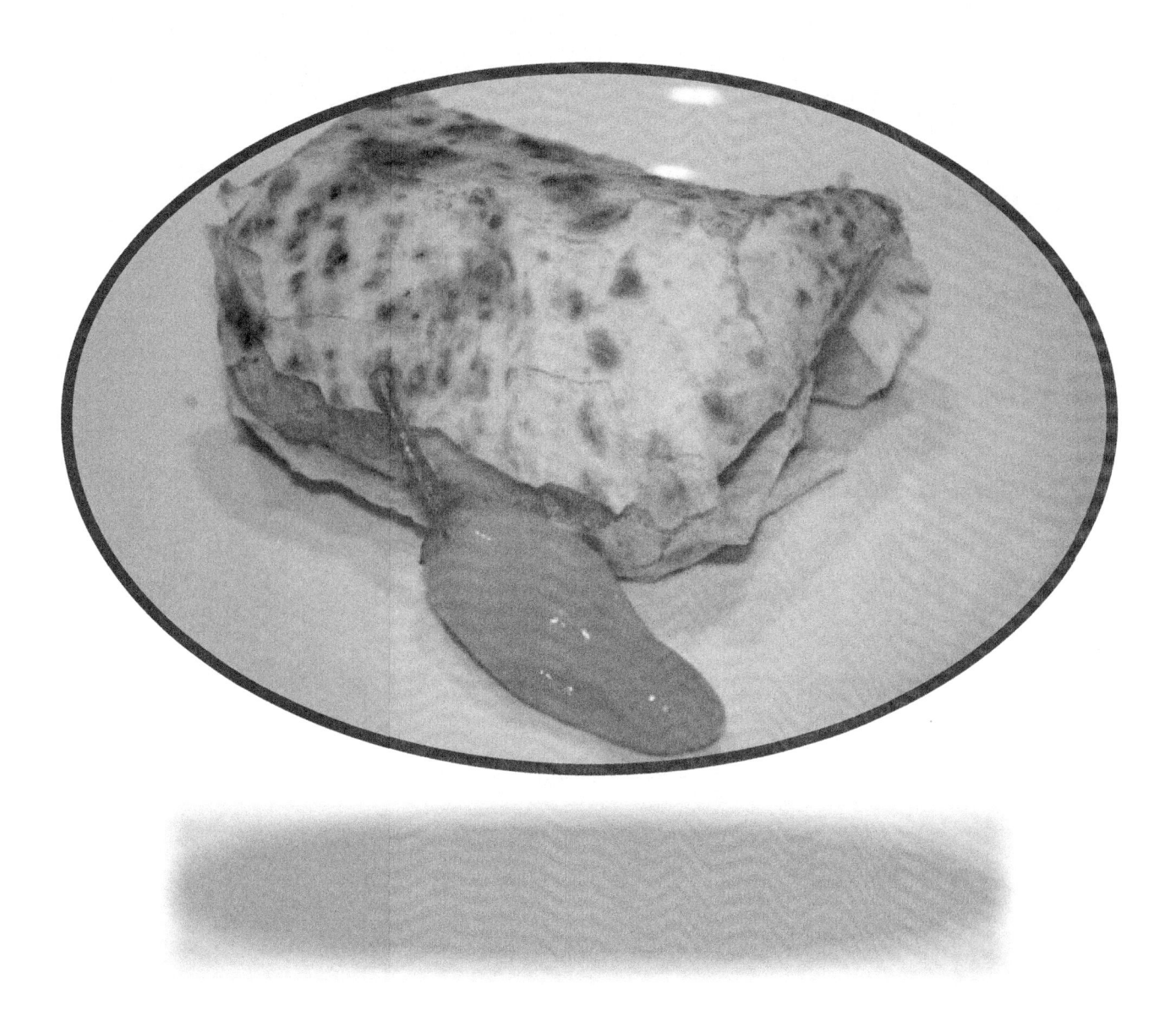

Turkey and Sweet Potato Wraps

Aqua Velvet

Ingredients

1 ounce rum

3/4 ounce vodka

1/2 ounce blue curacao

2 1/2 ounces pineapple juice

1 ounce prepared sweet-and-sour mix

1/4 ounce cream of coconut

ice (optional)

Directions

Pour all ingredients over ice in a hurricane glass.

Garnish with fresh pineapple wedge and or serve with a cocktail umbrella to spear maraschino cherry.

Aqua Velvet

Tropical Pineapple Banana Ice Cream

Ingredients

1/4 cup evaporated milk

1/4 cup fresh lemon juice

1 cup sugar

1/2 cup heavy cream

1 ripe banana, mashed (about 1/2 cup)

1/2 cup canned crushed pineapple, drained, reserving 2 T. of the juice

1 cup whole milk

Directions

In a large bowl, combine the evaporated milk, lemon juice, sugar, cream, banana, pineapple with reserved juice an the while milk.

Freeze the mixture in an ince-cream freezer according to the manufacturer's instructions.

Makes about 1 quart.

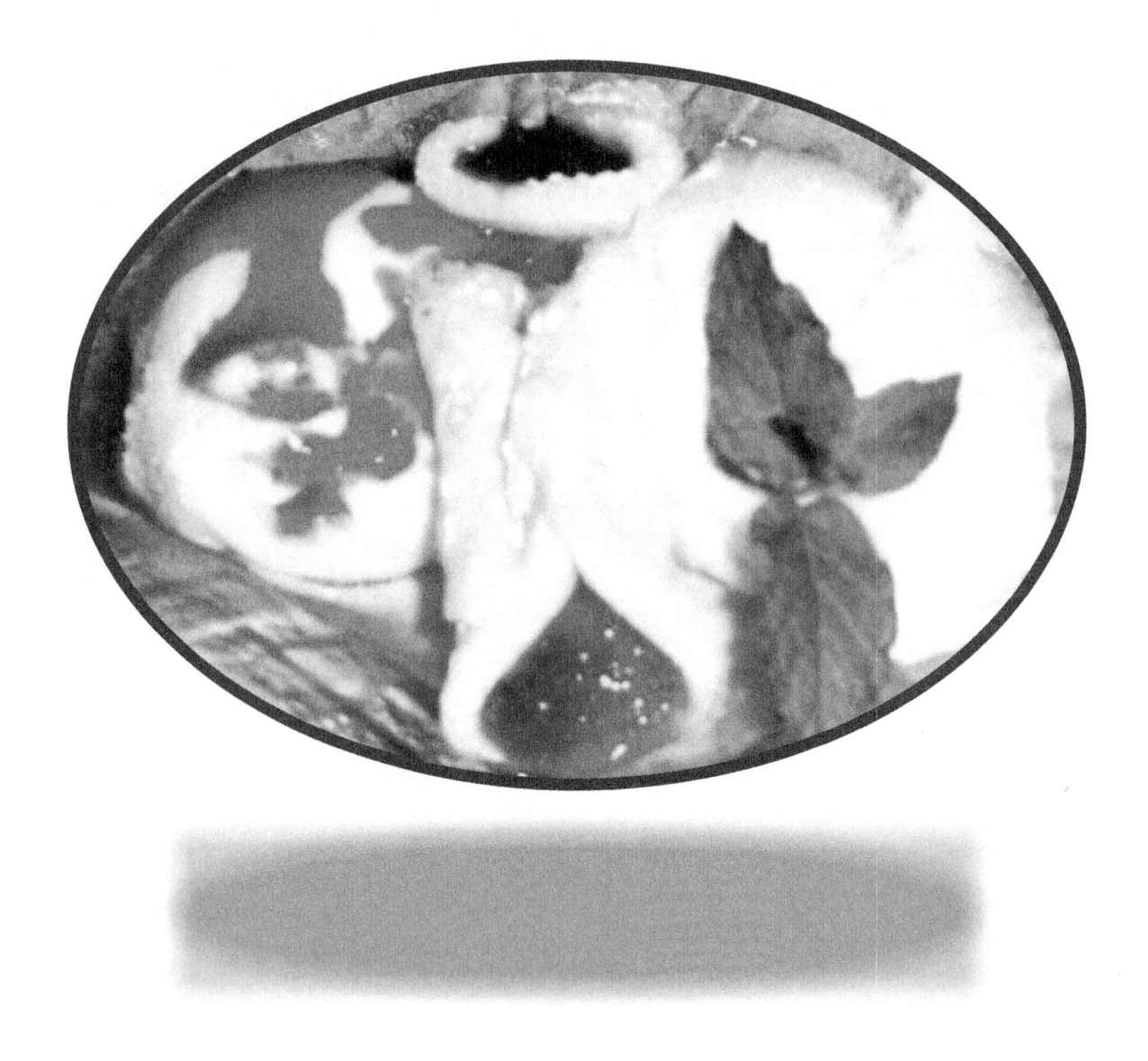

Tropical Pineapple Banana Ice Cream

Honolulu Lulu

Ingredients

2 ounces silver rum (light rum)

1 teaspoon grenadine

1/2 slice pineapple

1 1/2 ounces lemon juice

Directions

Blend all ingredients with 12 oz. glass of shaved ice in blender until liquid is semi-frozen.

Serve in a stemmed cocktail glass.

Honolulu Lulu

Grilled Apple Spice Trout Fillets

Ingredients

4 rainbow trout fillets (rainbow or any trout fillets)

2 tablespoons thawed apple juice concentrate (25 mL)

1 tablespoon Dijon mustard (15 mL)

1 teaspoon cider vinegar (5 mL)

1/2 teaspoon paprika (2 mL)

1/4 teaspoon pepper (1 mL)

1 pinch salt

Directions

Pat fillets dry; arrange, skin side down, on plate. In bowl, stir apple juice concentrate, mustard, vinegar, paprika, pepper and salt ; brush some of the sauce onto fillets.

Place fillets, skin side down, on greased grill over medium heat; close lid and cook, brushing once with remaining sauce, for 12 to 14 minutes or until fish flakes easily when tested with fork.

Grilled Apple Spice Trout Fillets

Watermelon Basil Vinaigrette

Ingredients

4 cups fresh watermelon, chopped and drained

1/4 cup red onion, diced small

2 tablespoons honey

1/4 cup champagne vinegar

3/4 cup canola oil

2 tablespoons fresh basil, chopped

1 tablespoon fresh parsley, chopped

salt and pepper

Directions

Add all ingredients to blender jar, cover and blend for until thoroughly blended.

Serve over your favorite salad.

Watermelon Basil Vinaigrette

Ravioli with Asparagus, Mint & Mascarpone

Ingredients

48 pieces cheese ravioli (fresh or frozen)

2 tablespoons olive oil

1-2 clove garlic, chopped

4 tablespoons mascarpone

2 tablespoons butter

1 cup chicken stock (or water)

1 bunch asparagus, chopped into 2 inch pieces (about 12 stalks)

1/2 cup of chopped mint

salt and pepper, to taste

parmigiano-reggiano cheese, to taste

Directions

Heat olive oil and garlic.

Add the asparagus and sauté for 2 to 3 minutes.

Stir in the butter and add the chicken stock.

Let this sauté while cooking the ravioli.

Cook ravioli in a large pot of salted boiling water for a few minutes until they float to the top.

Drain and gently add to the sauce.

Add the mascarpone & stir until incorporated.

Garnish with a dollop of mascarpone and fresh mint leaves.

Sprinkle with parmigiano reggiano and serve immediately.

Ravioli with Asparagus, Mint & Mascarpone

Wild Mango and Mustard Seed Salad

Ingredients

4 small ripe mangoes or 1 large ripe mango

1/2 tablespoon peanut oil

1 teaspoon black mustard seeds

4 curry leaves or 4 basil leaves, thinly sliced

2 dried red chilies, stalks pinched off and seeds shaken out or 1/2 teaspoon red chili pepper flakes

Directions

Peel the mangoes, remove the pits and cube the flesh.

Heat the oil in a wok or small saucepan and fry the mustard seeds until they pop.

Reduce the heat and add the curry leaves and the chilis.

Pour this oil with the spices into the mangoes. Mix lightly. Let the salad cool and serve at room temperature.

Wild Mango and Mustard Seed Salad

Grilled Rum Peaches with Mascarpone Cheese & Orange Blossom

Ingredients

2 ripe peaches

2 tablespoons honey, plus extra for serving

2 ounces mascarpone cheese, at room temperature

5 tablespoons butter

1/4 cup brown sugar

1/4 cup dark rum

1 teaspoon cinnamon

1/4 teaspoon salt

Directions

Combine all ingredients for the rum marinade in a stove-top pan on medium high heat. Reduce heat and let simmer for 7-8 minutes, stirring occasionally. Remove from heat and let cool.

Prepare peaches by cutting them in half and removing the pits. Place the peaches in a glass dish top with rum marinade. Marinate for 30 minutes to 4 hours.

Grill, cut side down for 3-4 minutes, then flip for another 5 minutes. Remove from grill and top with mascarpone cheese and drizzle with honey!

Grilled Rum Peaches with Mascarpone Cheese & Orange Blossom

Battered and Baked Sage Leaves

Ingredients

1 tablespoon olive oil

20-30 fresh sage leaves, the largest you can find

1 egg, plus

2 egg whites or 1/2 cup egg substitute, lightly beaten

salt and black pepper

1/3 cup flour or 1/3 cup fine toasted breadcrumbs

Directions

Preheat oven to 400 degrees F.

Line a baking sheet with tin foil and lightly oil with olive oil.

Beat the egg and egg whites or the egg subsitute with a fork and set to one side.

Put the flour or bread crumbs in a bowl and add some salt and a generous grinding of black pepper.

Now, dip the sage leaves one by one in the egg mixture, coat with the flour or bread crumbs and shake off any excess.

Lay on the baking sheet and finish the rest of the leaves.

Sprinkle a bit more salt and pepper on top of the leaves and then bake for 10-12 minutes, until nicely crisp and browned.

Serve immediately with your choice of dip or as a garnish.

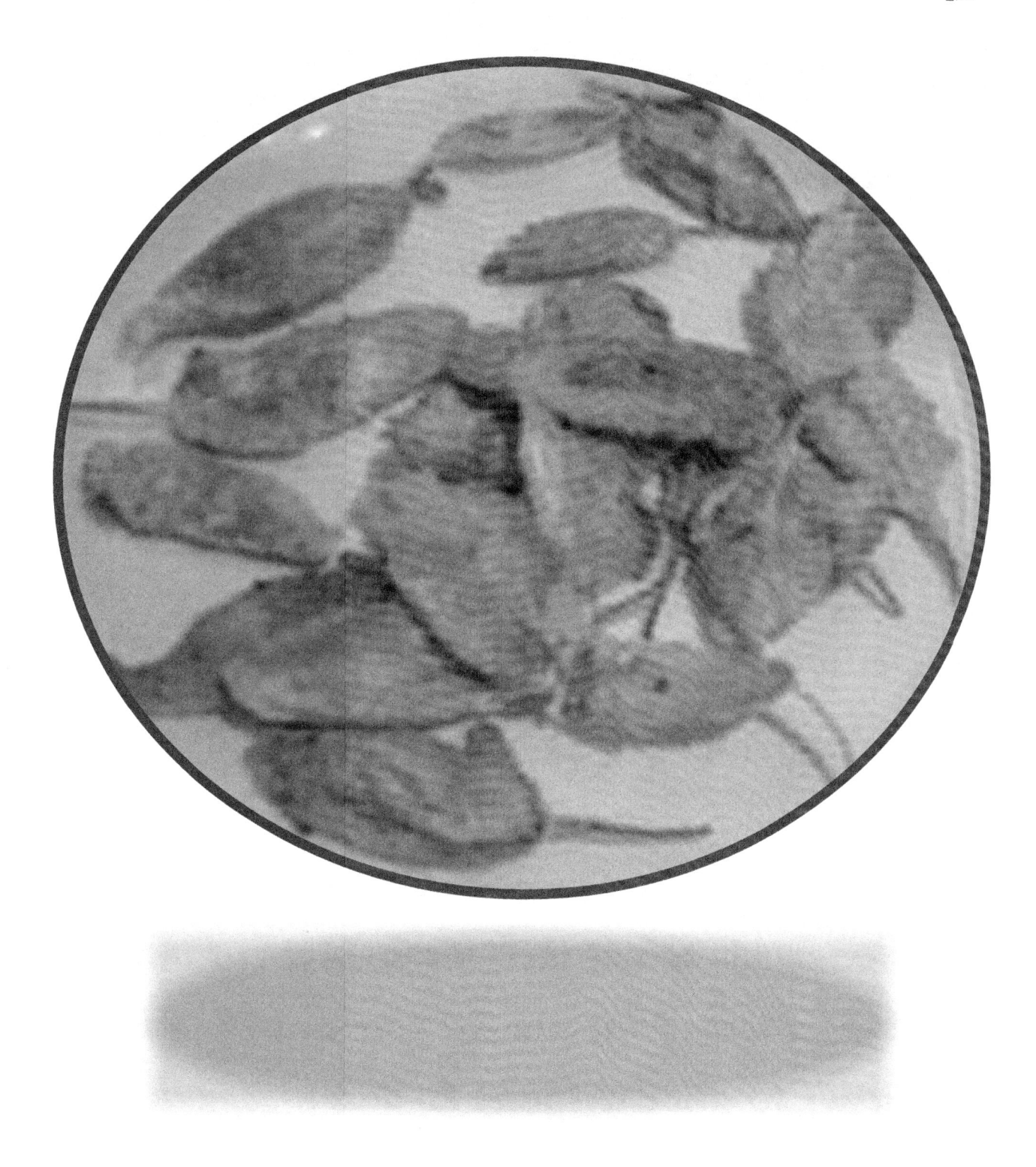

Battered and Baked Sage Leaves

Caramel Grilled Pineapple Sundaes

Ingredients

1 pineapple (fresh and ripe)

1 (10 ounce) jar caramel ice cream topping (You will have plenty left)

1 quart vanilla ice cream (also, you'll have some left)

Directions

Peel, core, and slice pineapple into 3/4 inch to 1 inch thick rings. If your pineapple is already cored and sliced in a way that makes it impossible to cut into rings, just cut into big wedges. Pieces that are cut too small make it difficult to grill without losing pieces in the grill, as the pineapple will soften somewhat.

Grill on a lightly oiled BBQ grill grate over medium to high heat, turning once, until the pineapple has nice grill marks, is warm, and slightly softened. Time will vary depending on your grill, but your eyes and your nose will tell you when it's ready!

Warm caramel ice cream topping in microwave according to package directions.

Assemble sundaes by placing a portion of pineapple in the bottom of each bowl. Top with a large scoop of vanilla ice cream, end drizzle a large spoonful of warm caramel topping over the top, and serve immediately.

Caramel Grilled Pineapple Sundaes

Coffee Barbecue Sauce

Ingredients

1 cup strong coffee

1/4 cup cider vinegar

1 teaspoon crushed garlic

1 teaspoon chili powder

1 1/2 cups catsup

1/2 cup Worcestershire sauce

1/2 cup dark brown sugar

Directions

Combine all ingredients in a large saucepan and simmer for 5 minutes.

Baste onto your meat while it's on the grill.

Refrigerate extra sauce.

Coffee Barbecue Sauce

White Cactus

Ingredients

1 ounce tequila

ginger ale

1 dash fresh lime juice

lime wedge

Directions

Pour ingredients over ice and garnish with lime wedge.

White Cactus

Pepper Jack Mac Salad

Ingredients

1 lb elbow macaroni or 1 lb cavatappi pasta

1 cup frozen corn, defrosted

1 red bell pepper, chopped

1 small red onion, chopped

4 celery ribs, chopped

8 ounces monterey jack pepper cheese, diced

2 tablespoons red wine vinegar, eyeball it

1/4 cup extra virgin olive oil, eyeball it

1 cup tomatillo salsa (mild, green) or 1 cup chipotle salsa (hot, smoky red)

2 tablespoons cilantro leaves, chopped or 2 tablespoons flat leaf parsley

salt and black pepper

Directions

Bring water to a boil, salt it and add pasta.

While pasta water is coming up to a boil and cooking, combine corn, pepper, onion and celery in a bowl with pepper Jack cheese. Season the veggies with salt and pepper.

Run pasta under cold water to cool it and drain it well. Add pasta to vegetables and cheese.

Place vinegar in a small bowl and whisk in extra-virgin olive oil, then fold in salsa. Pour sauce over salad and toss to coat evenly. Garnish salad with cilantro or parsley and serve.

Pepper Jack Mac Salad

Maple Pepper Steaks

Ingredients

1/2 cup maple syrup

1/4 cup olive oil

1 tablespoon pepper

1 tablespoon thyme, chopped

4 garlic cloves, peeled

1/2 teaspoon kosher salt

4 (8 ounce) beef tenderloin steaks (1 1/2 inch thick)

Directions

Combine all ingredients, except for he steaks in a blender and process until blended.

In a bowl or marinating dish combine beef with half of the marinade/sauce and let stand for at least 30 minutes or up to 4 hours. Remove steaks from marinade and discard.

Grill steaks, basting with remaining sauce until done.

Maple Pepper Steaks

Alouette Potato Salad

Ingredients

4 -5 medium red potatoes (cooked and cooled)

1 tablespoon chives, chopped

3 tablespoons red peppers, chopped

2 tablespoons black olives, chopped

1 alouette aioli

1 (12 ounce) bag mixed salad greens

Directions

Cut potatoes in half.

Place potatoes, scallions, chives, red peppers, and black olives in bowl.

Toss with Alouette Aioli Sauce.

Serve on a bed of salad greens.

Aioli Sauce.

1 pkg.(6.5 oz.) Alouette Garlic & Herbs Spreadable Cheese

6 tablespoons Olive oil.

2 tablespoons Vinegar (recommend balsamic).

1 teaspoons Shallots, minced.

Aioli Directions:.

Place Alouette Garlic & Herbs Spreadable Cheese in medium sized bowl.

In another bowl, whisk together olive oil, vinegar and shallots until well blended.

Gradually add the vinaigrette mixture to the cheese creating a delicious sauce.

Alouette Potato Salad

Seafood Risotto

Ingredients

2 pints vegetable stock (made up-kept warm or hot)

100 g butter, approx

1 medium onion, finely chopped (add another if you like)

1 garlic clove, crushed (minced garlic will be fine)

500 g fish (prawns, calamari, mussels etc)

spring onion (optional)

white wine

225 g arborio rice

Directions

prepare stock and keep warm/hot.

melt butter in big fry pan and add onions and garlic and cook about 5minutes.

add rice and stir continuously over a high heat for 2 minutes to allow grains to soften and then return to medium heat.

start to add the stock a ladle at a time, allow rice to absorb all stock before adding more, add some white wine.

keep doing this until all stock is used up, about 20-30 minutes.

add the seafood and cook about a further 3 minutes until heated through.

serve with chopped spring onions if desired.

Seafood Risotto

Crown of Roses

Ingredients

1 ounce Crown Royal whiskey

1/2 ounce Amaretto

1 ounce pineapple juice

1/4 ounce cranberry juice

3 dashes Angostura bitters

1 maraschino cherry (garnish, optional)

Directions

Fill a cocktail shaker two-thirds full of ice and add all of the ingredients.

Shake until well mixed and well chilled.

Strain into a chilled cocktail glass and add a cherry to garnish.

Crown of Roses

Chocolate Eclair Dessert

Ingredients

2 Jello Instant Vanilla Pudding Mix (small packages)

3 cups milk

8 ounces non-dairy whipped topping

1 (16 ounce) box graham crackers (you will have some leftovers)

1 (15 ounce) container chocolate frosting

Directions

Mix together vanilla pudding mix and milk.

Fold in whipped topping.

Line 9 x 13 pan with one layer of graham crackers.

Put half of the pudding mixture over the graham crackers.

Place a second layer of graham crackers over the pudding mixture.

Put the remaining pudding mixture over the graham crackers.

Place a third layer of graham crackers over the pudding mixture.

Heat the tub of frosting in the microwave for 30 seconds to soften. (Don't forget to remove the foil seal or you'll get fireworks).

Spread frosting on the top of the last layer of graham crackers.

Cover with plastic wrap and let set a couple hours or overnight in the refrigerator.

Cut in squares.

Chocolate Eclair Dessert

Southern Style Cinnamon Honey Chicken

Ingredients

3 lbs chicken, jointed in 8 pieces (make sure to use good quality chicken!)

1/2 cup flour

2 teaspoons salt

3/teaspoon good quality cinnamon

1/4 teaspoon turmeric

1/6/teaspoon black pepper

1/6 pinch freshly ground nutmeg

1 egg

2 tablespoons milk

1/3 cup dried crushed breadcrumbs

cooking spray

2 tablespoons oil (optional)

Directions

Preheat oven to 350 degrees F.

Spray a large roasting pan lightly with cooking spray.

Combine the flour with the salt, cinnamon, turmeric, black pepper, and a pinch nutmeg.

Coat the chicken pieces well with the flour mixture (you can use chicken with or without skin on - it's up to you).

Beat together the egg and milk; dredge the flour-coated chicken pieces in the egg mixture, then into the breadcrumbs.

Arrange pieces skin side up (if using pieces with skin) in the sprayed roasting pan, making sure that the pieces are not touching each other (if possible) to ensure they bake crispy; spray chicken pieces with oil spray or sprinkle with 2 tablespoons oil and place the chicken in the oven to bake.

While the chicken is baking, in a saucepan over medium low heat combine the butter, honey, pinches of cinnamon, and lemon juice.

After the chicken has baked for 25 minutes, pour the butter and honey mixture generously over the pieces.

Bake for an additional 15 minutes or until the juices run clear and the chicken is crisp and brown.

Note: if you'd like to add a bit of kick to the recipe, you can try a pinch or two of cayenne (to taste) in the honey sauce, or perhaps some red pepper flakes!

Southern Style Cinnamon Honey Chicken

Garlic Ricotta Stuffed Mushrooms

Ingredients

7 large white mushrooms, stems removed

5 garlic cloves, crushed

3 -4 tablespoons part-skim ricotta cheese

1/4 teaspoon salt

1/2 teaspoon cracked black pepper

1 tablespoon olive oil

4 tablespoons grated parmesan cheese

Directions

Preheat oven to 350°F.

Clean mushrooms, remove stems.

Chop stems, and the one extra mushroom.

Heat olive oil in sauté pan.

Add chopped stems and the one extra mushroom.

Halfway through cooking add crushed garlic, salt and pepper.

Remove from heat and allow to cool slightly in a small mixing bowl.

Add ricotta and 2 tablespoons grated Parmesan.

Fill caps with the cheese mixture and place on a cookie sheet that has been sprayed with cooking spray.

Sprinkle remaining Parmesan on top.

Bake for approx 20-25 minutes.

Garlic Ricotta Stuffed Mushrooms

Blackberry Coffee Cake

Ingredients

1 1/2 cups all-purpose flour

2 teaspoons baking powder

1 cup sugar

1 large egg, beaten

3/4 cup milk

3 tablespoons butter, melted

1 teaspoon vanilla extract

1/2 cup sugar

1/2 pint fresh blackberries, rinsed and drained

Directions

Preheat oven to 350°F.

Mix together flour, baking powder and the 1 cup of sugar.

Add the beaten egg, milk, melted butter and vanilla; mix until smooth.

Mix together the 1/2 cup sugar and the blackberries, stirring to coat the berries evenly; set aside.

Pour cake mixture into a well-greased 9" round cake pan.

Top cake batter with sugared berries; swirl around gently with a spoon, leaving some on top.

Bake at 350° for 30 minutes or until a toothpick inserted in the middle of the cake comes out clean (if it hits a berry, try somewhere else).

Cool in pan on a wire rack.

Blackberry Coffee Cake

Five-Spices Chicken Wings

Ingredients

- 3 lbs chicken wings
- 2 tablespoons soy sauce
- 2 tablespoons hoisin sauce
- 2 tablespoons rice vinegar
- 1 tablespoon five-spice powder
- 1 tablespoon vegetable oil
- 1/2 teaspoon salt
- 1/2 teaspoon fresh black pepper
- 2 garlic cloves, finely minced
- 3 tablespoons liquid honey

Directions

Cut the tips of chicken wings and throw them away. Cut the chicken wings in two at the joints.

In a big bowl, mix remaining ingredients, except the honey.

Add chicken wings and flip to coat well.

Cover and let marinate 2 hours in the fridge. (You can do this step one day ahead and cover them. They will be good until the next day).

Put the barbecue to medium heat.

Put the chicken wings on a greased grill or in a grill basket.

Close the cover of barbecue and cook for about 25 minutes or until chicken wings are crispy and juice runs clear when poking with a fork. (MAKE SURE TO FLIP THEM SOMETIMES).

Baste chicken wings with honey, close cover of barbecue and keep cooking 3 minutes (flip them one time).

Five-Spices Chicken Wings

Tomato Beef Chow Mein

Ingredients

Marinade

2 tablespoons soy sauce

1 tablespoon sugar

2 tablespoons ginger, minced

1 garlic clove, minced

1 tablespoon sherry wine

1 tablespoon sesame seed oil

2 teaspoons cornstarch

Chow Mein

1/2lb flank steak, sliced thin against grain

1 lb chow mein noodles

1 medium onion

1 green bell pepper

2 medium tomatoes, very ripe and taste

1 tablespoon oil

frying oil

Sauce

1 1/2 tablespoons cornstarch

1 tablespoon sugar

1 tablespoon vinegar

2 tablespoons sherry wine

1/2 teaspoon salt

2 tablespoons catsup

1 cup beef broth

Directions

Thinly slice beef. Mix marinade and beef together. Set aside.

Mix sauce ingredients and set aside.

Cook mein noodles in boiling water for 1-3 minutes. They cook fast. Rinse well with cold water and drain. Toss with 1 tablespoon oil so noodles won't stick together. Heat large nonstick skillet, glaze with oil and pan fry 1/4 of the noodles at a time. Put in very low oven to keep warm.

Thinly slice onion and pepper set a side.

Cut tomatoes into 1/2" wide wedges and set aside.

Heat wok. add 1 tablespoon oil, swirl and add onions and peppers. Stir fry 2 minutes, then turn out of pan.

Drain marinade off meat.

Add 1 tablespoon oil to wok, swirl, add meat. After 1 minute, add tomatoes and stir fry w/meat gently.

Return veggies to pan and add sauce. Cook stirring until it boils and thickens. Sauce needs to be thick enough to glazes the noodles with out drowning them.

Pour over noodles and enjoy.

Tomato Beef Chow Mein

Apple Juice Frosty

Ingredients

1 cup vanilla ice cream

2 cups apple juice

1 dash cinnamon (optional)

Directions

Combine ice cream and apple juice.

Beat until foamy.

Pour into glasses.

Top each serving with a sprinkle of cinnamon.

Apple Juice Frosty

The Blizzard

Ingredients

8 ounces apple juice

4 ounces pineapple juice

4 ounces orange juice

2 ounces cranberry juice

2 ounces grapefruit juice

2 ounces vodka

grenadine (optional)

Directions

Stir all ingredients together.

Color with grenadine if desired.

Serve over ice in tall, frosted glasses

The Blizzard

Good Thyme Lamb Chops

Ingredients

8 lamb loin chops

3 tablespoons chopped fresh thyme

1 tablespoon fresh lemon juice

3 cloves garlic, minced

2 tablespoons olive oil

2 teaspoons salt

1/2 teaspoon black pepper

Directions

Place lamb chops in glass dish. Combine remaining ingredients and rub into the meat on both sides.

Let stand, covered, for 1-2 hours at room temperature.

Prepare a hot grill. Grill about 15 minutes, until browned on the outside, but still pink in the middle.

Good Thyme Lamb Chops

Shopping list...

Printed in Great Britain
by Amazon